Thanks to my family and friends, for your continuous love and support!

SPECIAL THANKS AND ACKNOWLEDGEMENT
Daniel and Ashley
– the other half of my heart –

HOW TO USE
Journal to Wellness

Journal to Wellness: Create the Life YOU Desire and Deserve is a spin-off from my first book *BREAK FREE: 52 Tips to Escape from Your Self-Imposed Prison* where I challenged readers to get out of their own way by doing various activities that helped them to take an introspective look at their life.

Writing has always been the vehicle that I have used to help me cope with life challenges. Whenever, I am feeling down, overwhelmed or overall, not in a good space for whatever reason – writing usually makes me feel better. Fifty-five percent of the time it does not solve the problem, but it puts the situation in perspective and/or just gives me a means to vent.

According to *Psychology Today*, journaling has numerous benefits such as helping one to:
- Take a step back and evaluate ones thoughts, emotions, and behavior
- Identify solutions
- Transform negative energy to positive by allowing one to look at a situation from a different perspective
- See other peoples' perspectives alongside our own

Downside of Journaling
Despite its positive impact, journaling can be counter-productive. The main reason being, one can get stuck in a negative space - wallowing in self-pity and blaming oneself and others - instead of using the writing process to gain clarity, insight and possibly, a new perspective.

It's because of this negative ramification that I developed a format to journaling called *Journal to Wellness*© that I and others have used that has helped us tremendously.

The following is the format that you may use to guide your journaling that will not only benefit you but others.

1. **I am feeling...**
   Write a brief summary of what is happening (include how you are feeling). *Make this three paragraphs at the most.*

2. **I am grateful...**
   List at least 1 thing you're grateful for. *(As you go through this journaling experience, try to identify a new thing you are grateful for each time. You will be so surprised about the many things that you may have taken for granted.)*

3. **I will take care of myself by ...**
   If you are in a __negative__ space emotionally or physically
   - List at least one POSITIVE thing that you will do to change how you are feeling or help you to cope.

   If you are in a __positive__ space emotionally or physically
   - List at least one POSITIVE thing that you will do to maintain or enhance how you are feeling.

4. **I will do at least one act of kindness for someone today.**
   Record the act of kindness that you will do.

Feedback about the *Journal to Wellness* © Format
I tested this format among a group of my friends who committed to journal for one month using the format I created. The feedback was as follows:

- *"It helped me to look at my life differently because I came to realize that no matter what is happening in my life, I always have something to be grateful for."*

- *"Identifying one act of kindness to do for someone else each day took the focus off of me and help me to think of others."*

- *"Using this format stopped me from wallowing in self-pity."*

- *"It reminded me that I am as important as the other person and it's important to be kind to myself."*

- *"It helped me to see that I spent a lot of time in my head."*

- *"Seeing my thoughts on paper was an eye-opener. I did not realize that I beat up on myself so badly!"*

Happy journaling!
Faith

OTHER WAYS TO USE
Journal to Wellness©

If journaling is not your thing, and for some people, it is not; *Journal to Wellness* can still add value to your life.

1. **INSPIRATION:** It contains quotes geared at encouraging and motivating you as you go through your busy day!

2. **CHALLENGES HOW YOU THINK:** It also includes questions to challenge you to step outside of your comfort zone and taking steps towards fulfilling your full potential.

3. **HELPS YOU TO PRIORITIZE:** It helps you to put your life in perspective by focusing on the many things that you have to be grateful for.

4. **RECORD NOTES:** Great way to record notes at meetings.

5. **KEEP TRACK OF WHAT YOU HAVE TO DO:** If you are like me and still use a physical book to record your To Do List, this is an all-inclusive package!

SMILE

It could make the world of a difference!

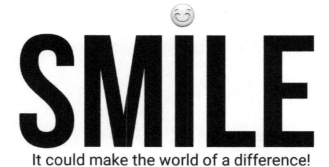

Date: ____________________

I am feeling…

I am grateful for…

_____

_____

_____

_____

_____

_____

_____

I will take care of myself by …

_____

_____

_____

_____

_____

_____

I will do at least one act of kindness for someone today.

_____

_____

_____

_____

_____

_____

"Let your smile change the world but don't let the world change your smile." - Unknown -

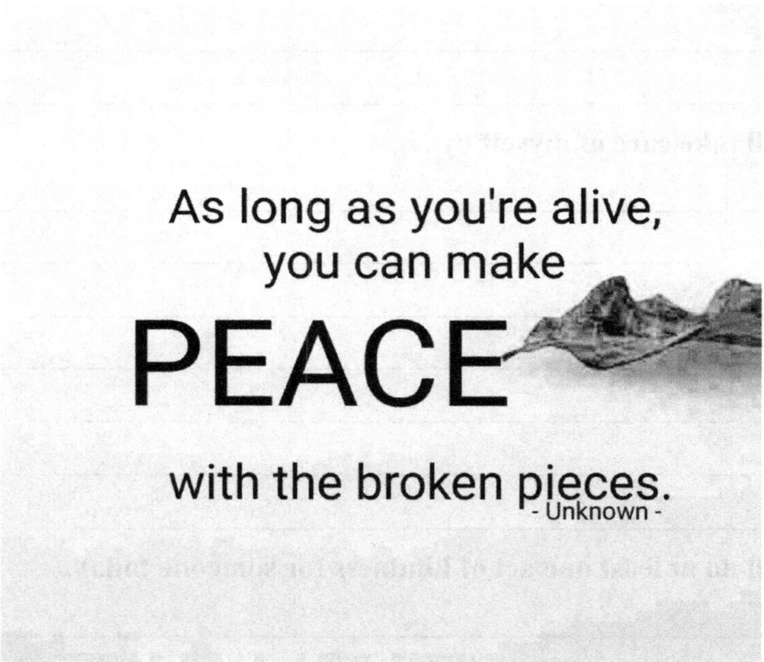
As long as you're alive,
you can make
PEACE
with the broken pieces.
- Unknown -

Date: _____

I am feeling…

_____
_____
_____
_____
_____
_____
_____
_____
_____
_____
_____
_____
_____
_____
_____
_____
_____
_____
_____
_____
_____
_____
_____
_____

I am grateful for...

_____
_____
_____
_____
_____
_____

I will take care of myself by ...

_____
_____
_____
_____
_____
_____

I will do at least one act of kindness for someone today.

_____
_____
_____
_____
_____
_____

"Remember, whatever you focus upon, increases!"

PROSPERITY IS KNOWING WHO YOU ARE LOVING IT AND DOING WHAT YOU LOVE.

- Unknown -

Date: _____

I am feeling…

_____

_____

_____

_____

_____

_____

_____

_____

_____

_____

_____

_____

_____

_____

_____

_____

_____

_____

_____

_____

_____

I am grateful for...

_____

_____

_____

_____

_____

_____

_____

I will take care of myself by ...

_____

_____

_____

_____

_____

_____

I will do at least one act of kindness for someone today.

_____

_____

_____

_____

_____

_____

Your big picture will never be a masterpiece if you ignore the tiny brushstrokes." – Andy Andrews -

True forgiveness is when you can say,

"Thank you for that experience."

- Oprah Winfrey -

Date: _____

I am feeling...

_____

_____

_____

_____

_____

_____

_____

_____

_____

_____

_____

_____

_____

_____

_____

_____

_____

_____

_____

_____

_____

_____

_____

_____

I am grateful for...

_____

_____

_____

_____

_____

_____

_____

I will take care of myself by ...

_____

_____

_____

_____

_____

_____

I will do at least one act of kindness for someone today.

_____

_____

_____

_____

_____

_____

_____

_____

Identify someone who you have to forgive.
Don't forget to include yourself.

YOUR Perception is Reality!
Is this glass half full or half empty?
www.discoveranewfuture.com

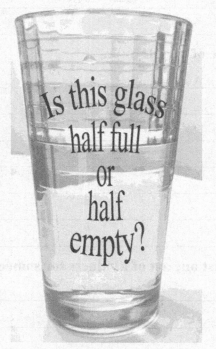

Date: _____

I am feeling...

_____
_____
_____
_____
_____
_____
_____
_____
_____
_____
_____
_____
_____
_____
_____
_____
_____
_____
_____
_____
_____
_____
_____
_____

I am grateful for...

_____

_____

_____

_____

_____

_____

_____

I will take care of myself by ...

_____

_____

_____

_____

_____

_____

I will do at least one act of kindness for someone today.

_____

_____

_____

_____

_____

_____

Your PERCEPTION *about life is your* REALITY!
Is your glass half empty or full?

Sometimes
the path can
seem so long... & loney.

But remember
YOU'RE NEVER ALONE.

Date: ____________________

I am feeling…

I am grateful for...

_____

_____

_____

_____

_____

_____

_____

I will take care of myself by ...

_____

_____

_____

_____

_____

_____

I will do at least one act of kindness for someone today.

_____

_____

_____

_____

_____

_____

_____

"Dream as if you'll live forever, live as if you'll die tomorrow."
– Jean Dean -

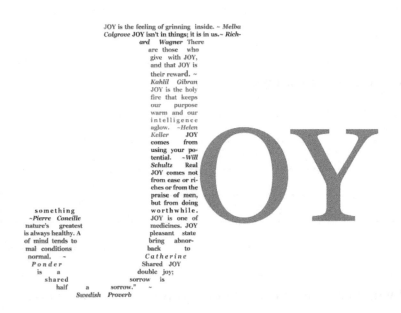

JOY is the feeling of grinning inside. ~ *Melba Colgrove* JOY isn't in things; it is in us.~ *Richard Wagner* There are those who give with JOY, and that JOY is their reward. ~ *Kahlil Gibran* JOY is the holy fire that keeps our purpose warm and our intelligence aglow. ~*Helen Keller* JOY comes from using your potential. ~*Will Schultz* Real JOY comes not from ease or riches or from the praise of men, but from doing worthwhile. JOY is one of medicines. JOY pleasant state bring abnormal back to *Catherine* Shared JOY double joy; sorrow is sorrow." ~ *Swedish Proverb*

something ~*Pierre Concille* nature's greatest is always healthy. A of mind tends to mal conditions normal. ~ *Ponder* is a shared half a

Choose a JOY quote that inspires you? *(Write it below)*

_____

_____

Date: _____

I am feeling...

_____

_____

_____

_____

_____

_____

_____

_____

_____

_____

_____

_____

_____

_____

_____

_____

_____

_____

_____

_____

_____

_____

_____

_____

I am grateful for...

_____

_____

_____

_____

_____

_____

_____

I will take care of myself by ...

_____

_____

_____

_____

_____

_____

I will do at least one act of kindness for someone today.

_____

_____

_____

_____

_____

_____

_____

"Find JOY in the ordinary."
– Unknown -

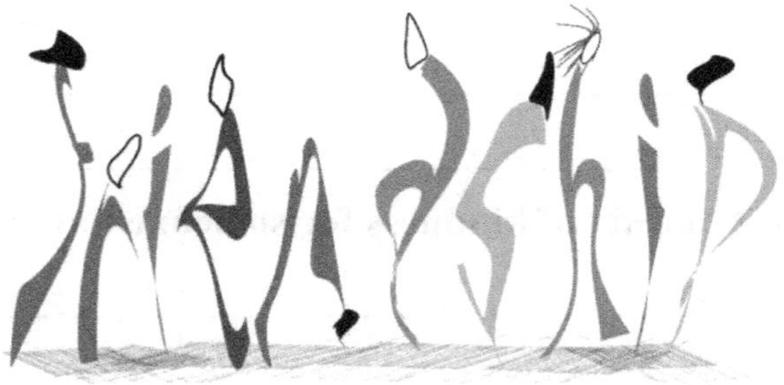
friendship

"Good friends are like stars…
You don't always see them, but you know they
are always there." - Unknown -

Date: ____________________

I am feeling…

I am grateful for...

_____

_____

_____

_____

_____

_____

I will take care of myself by ...

_____

_____

_____

_____

_____

_____

I will do at least one act of kindness for someone today.

_____

_____

_____

_____

_____

_____

_Reach out to a friend you have not seen or heard
from in a long time._

"EVERYTHING
you want in
LIFE
is waiting for you outside of your
COMFORT ZONE!"
Anthony Fernando

Date: _____

I am feeling...

_____

_____

_____

_____

_____

_____

_____

_____

_____

_____

_____

_____

_____

_____

_____

_____

_____

_____

_____

_____

_____

_____

I am grateful for…

_____

_____

_____

_____

_____

_____

_____

I will take care of myself by …

_____

_____

_____

_____

_____

_____

I will do at least one act of kindness for someone today.

_____

_____

_____

_____

_____

_____

_____

In order to grow, we have to step outside of our comfort zone.
What will you do today to stretch yourself?

"People come into your life for **a reason, a season or a lifetime**. When you figure out which it is, you know exactly what to do."
- Michelle Ventor -

Date: _____

I am feeling…

_____

_____

_____

_____

_____

_____

_____

_____

_____

_____

_____

_____

_____

_____

_____

_____

_____

_____

_____

_____

_____

_____

_____

_____

I am grateful for...

_____

_____

_____

_____

_____

_____

_____

I will take care of myself by ...

_____

_____

_____

_____

_____

_____

I will do at least one act of kindness for someone today.

_____

_____

_____

_____

_____

_____

_____

Insert the name of someone who has made a difference in your life.

_____

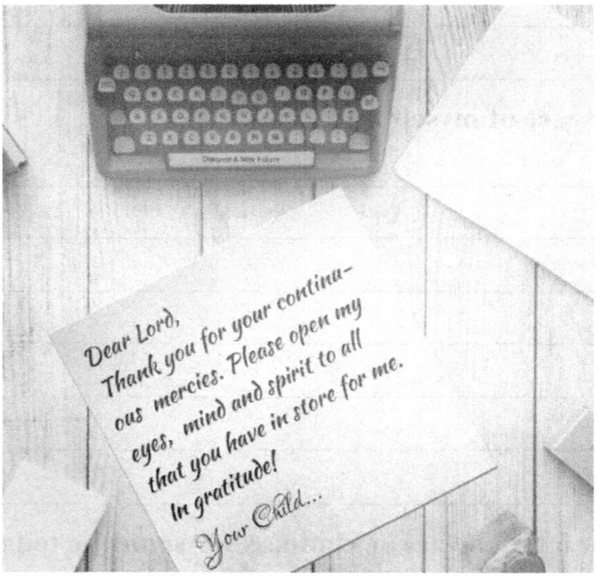
Dear Lord,
Thank you for your continu-
ous mercies. Please open my
eyes, mind and spirit to all
that you have in store for me.
In gratitude!
Your Child...

Date: ____________________

I am feeling…

I am grateful for…

_____

_____

_____

_____

_____

_____

I will take care of myself by …

_____

_____

_____

_____

_____

I will do at least one act of kindness for someone today.

_____

_____

_____

_____

_____

"When we love and accept ourselves, we navigate life more authentically." – Faith Saunders –

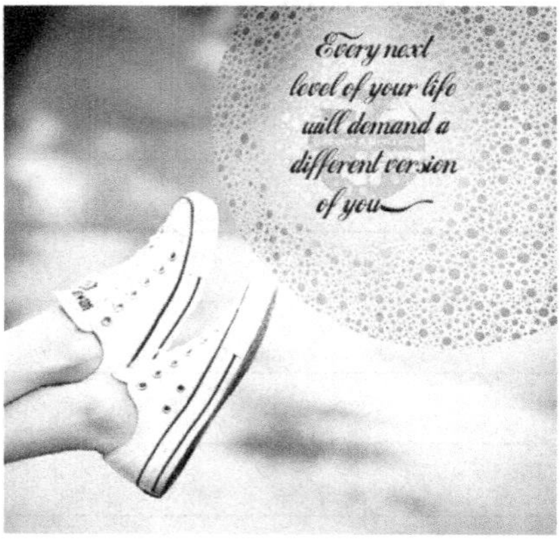
Every next
level of your life
will demand a
different version
of you

Every next level of your life will demand a different version of you!
– Unknown –

Are you prepared to do what it takes?

Date: ____________________

I am feeling…

I am grateful for...

_____

_____

_____

_____

_____

_____

_____

I will take care of myself by ...

_____

_____

_____

_____

_____

_____

I will do at least one act of kindness for someone today.

_____

_____

_____

_____

_____

_____

_____

_What changes do you have to make with your thoughts and/or
behaviors to transition to the next phase of your life?_

"When we LET GO OF WHAT OTHERS THINK and own our story, we gain access to our WORTHINESS."

- Brené Brown -

Date: ____________________

I am feeling…

I am grateful for...

_____

_____

_____

_____

_____

_____

_____

I will take care of myself by ...

_____

_____

_____

_____

_____

_____

_____

I will do at least one act of kindness for someone today.

_____

_____

_____

_____

_____

_____

_____

"When we deny the story, it defines us. When we own the story we can write a brave new ending." – Brene Brown -

TAKE THE ATTITUDE OF A STUDENT

Photo: Melissa Jill

NEVER be too big to ask questions
NEVER know too much to learn
something new.

Og Mandino

Date: _____

I am feeling…

_____

_____

_____

_____

_____

_____

_____

_____

_____

_____

_____

_____

_____

_____

_____

_____

_____

_____

_____

_____

_____

_____

_____

I am grateful for...

_____

_____

_____

_____

_____

_____

I will take care of myself by ...

_____

_____

_____

_____

_____

_____

I will do at least one act of kindness for someone today.

_____

_____

_____

_____

_____

_____

What's your attitude towards life?

As a single footstep will not make a path on the earth, so a single thought will not make a pathway in the mind.

To make a deep physical path, we walk again and again. To make a deep mental path, we must think over and over the kind of thoughts we wish to dominate our lives.

Henry David Thoreau

Date: ____________________

I am feeling…

I am grateful for...

_____

_____

_____

_____

_____

_____

_____

I will take care of myself by ...

_____

_____

_____

_____

_____

_____

I will do at least one act of kindness for someone today.

_____

_____

_____

_____

_____

_____

_____

"Think positively!"

Live your life so that at the end of the day, there are

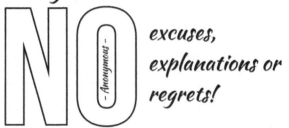

excuses, explanations or regrets!

CHECK POINT
Are you on track to achieving this end goal?

Date: ____________________

I am feeling…

I am grateful for...

_____

_____

_____

_____

_____

_____

_____

_____

I will take care of myself by ...

_____

_____

_____

_____

_____

_____

_____

I will do at least one act of kindness for someone today.

_____

_____

_____

_____

_____

_____

_____

_____

"Go confidently in the direction of your dreams. Live the life you've imagined." - Henry David Thoreau -

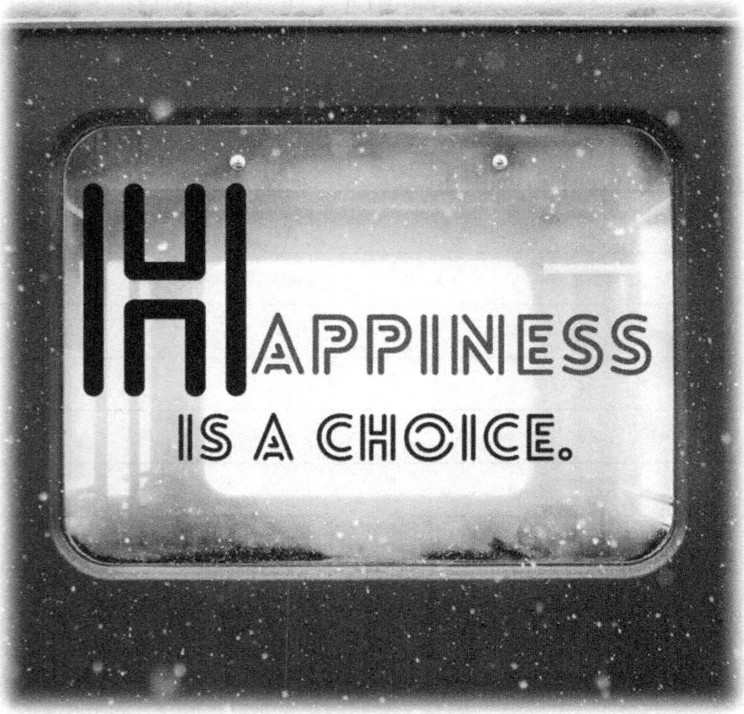
HAPPINESS
IS A CHOICE.

Date: _____

I am feeling…

_____
_____
_____
_____
_____
_____
_____
_____
_____
_____
_____
_____
_____
_____
_____
_____
_____
_____
_____
_____
_____
_____
_____
_____
_____
_____

I am grateful for…

_____

_____

_____

_____

_____

_____

_____

I will take care of myself by …

_____

_____

_____

_____

_____

_____

I will do at least one act of kindness for someone today.

_____

_____

_____

_____

_____

_____

_____

"Happiness is an inside job. It's one responsibility you should not delegate."- Faith Saunders -

SURRENDER

"It was the moment I accepted, no, it was the moment when I flat-out fully SURRENDERED, that everything began to flow to me."

- Carol Egan -

Date: ____________________

I am feeling…

I am grateful for...

_____

_____

_____

_____

_____

_____

I will take care of myself by ...

_____

_____

_____

_____

_____

_____

I will do at least one act of kindness for someone today.

_____

_____

_____

_____

_____

_____

_____

"Live your life as if everything is rigged in your favor." – Rumi –

YOU HAVE TO

BE

BEFORE YOU CAN

DO

AND DO BEFORE YOU CAN

HAVE

Zig Ziglar

Date: _____

I am feeling…

_____
_____
_____
_____
_____
_____
_____
_____
_____
_____
_____
_____
_____
_____
_____
_____
_____
_____
_____
_____
_____
_____
_____
_____
_____
_____
_____

I am grateful for...

_____
_____
_____
_____
_____
_____
_____

I will take care of myself by ...

_____
_____
_____
_____
_____
_____

I will do at least one act of kindness for someone today.

_____
_____
_____
_____
_____
_____

"Be patient with yourself."

Believe in yourself. Have **FAITH** in your abilities! Without a humble but reasonable confidence in your own powers, you cannot be successful or happy. ~ *Norman Vincent Peale* ~ Fear knocked at the door. **FAITH** answered. No one was there. ~ *Author Unknown* Where there is **FAITH**, there is love; Where there is love, there is peace; Where there is peace, there is God; And where there is God; there is no need. ~ *Leo Tolstoy* ~ Lord, I don't ask for a **FAITH** that would move yonder mountain. I can take enough dynamite and move it, if it needs movin'. I pray, Lord, for enough **FAITH** to move me. ~ *Norman Allen* ~ I tell you the truth, if you have FAITH as small as a mustard seed, you can say to this mountain, 'Move from here to there' and it will move. ~ *Matthew 17:20* ~ FAITH goes up the stairs love has built and looks out the window which hope has opened. ~ *Charles Spurgeon* ~ Now **FAITH** is being sure of what we hope for and certain of what we do not see. ~ *Hebrews 11:1* ~ "You block your dream when you allow your fear to grow bigger than your **FAITH**." ~ *Mary Manin Morrissey* ~ **Keepsakes by Faith**

aith

Choose your favorite FAITH quote and write it below.

_____

_____

Date: ____________________

I am feeling…

I am grateful for...

_____

_____

_____

_____

_____

_____

_____

I will take care of myself by ...

_____

_____

_____

_____

_____

_____

I will do at least one act of kindness for someone today.

_____

_____

_____

_____

_____

_____

What legacy do you want to leave behind?

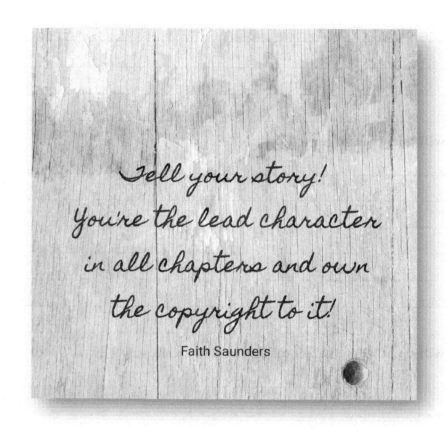

Tell your story!
You're the lead character
in all chapters and own
the copyright to it!

Faith Saunders

Date: _____

I am feeling...

_____
_____
_____
_____
_____
_____
_____
_____
_____
_____
_____
_____
_____
_____
_____
_____
_____
_____
_____
_____
_____
_____
_____
_____

I am grateful for...

_____

_____

_____

_____

_____

_____

_____

I will take care of myself by ...

_____

_____

_____

_____

_____

_____

I will do at least one act of kindness for someone today.

_____

_____

_____

_____

_____

_____

_____

“Fear knocked at the door. FAITH answered. No one was there.”
– Unknown -

*"TODAY, I will take my place at
the table of life because I have
a right to be here!"*

\- Unknown

Date: _____

I am feeling...

_____

_____

_____

_____

_____

_____

_____

_____

_____

_____

_____

_____

_____

_____

_____

_____

_____

_____

_____

_____

_____

_____

_____

I am grateful for...

_____

_____

_____

_____

_____

_____

_____

I will take care of myself by ...

_____

_____

_____

_____

_____

_____

I will do at least one act of kindness for someone today.

_____

_____

_____

_____

_____

REMEMBER, *"You're a child of the Universe, no less than the trees and the stars, you have a right to be here."* - Desiderata -

TURN YOUR

WOUNDS

INTO

WISDOM.

- Oprah Winfrey -

Date: _____

I am feeling…

_____

_____

_____

_____

_____

_____

_____

_____

_____

_____

_____

_____

_____

_____

_____

_____

_____

_____

_____

_____

_____

_____

_____

I am grateful for…

_____

_____

_____

_____

_____

_____

_____

I will take care of myself by …

_____

_____

_____

_____

_____

_____

I will do at least one act of kindness for someone today.

_____

_____

_____

_____

_____

_____

_____

"So go ahead. Fall down. The world looks different from the ground." - Oprah -

You can dance anywhere,
even if only in your heart.
~Author Unknown

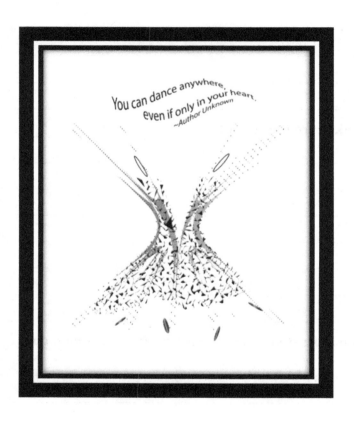

When was the last time you went dancing?

Date: _____

I am feeling…

_____

_____

_____

_____

_____

_____

_____

_____

_____

_____

_____

_____

_____

_____

_____

_____

_____

_____

_____

_____

_____

_____

_____

I am grateful for...

_____

_____

_____

_____

_____

_____

_____

I will take care of myself by ...

_____

_____

_____

_____

_____

_____

I will do at least one act of kindness for someone today.

_____

_____

_____

_____

_____

_____

_____

♫ _Dance! Dance! Dance!_ ♫

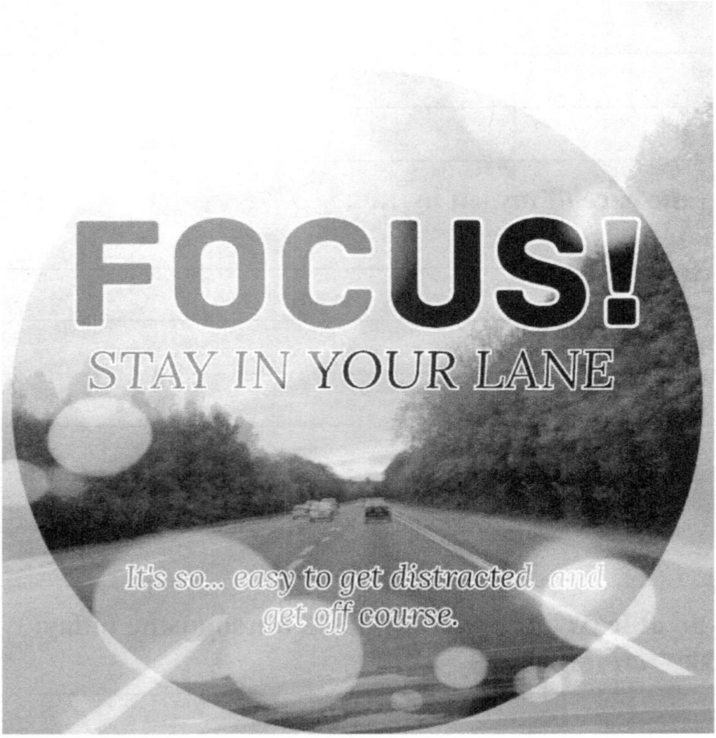
FOCUS!
STAY IN YOUR LANE
It's so... easy to get distracted and get off course.

Date: ____________________

I am feeling…

I am grateful for…

I will take care of myself by …

I will do at least one act of kindness for someone today.

Stay on

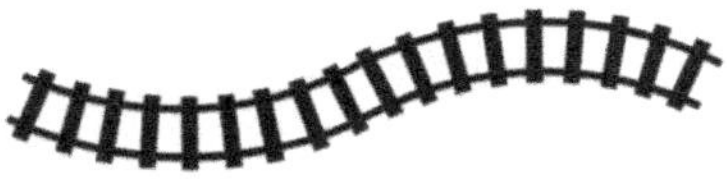

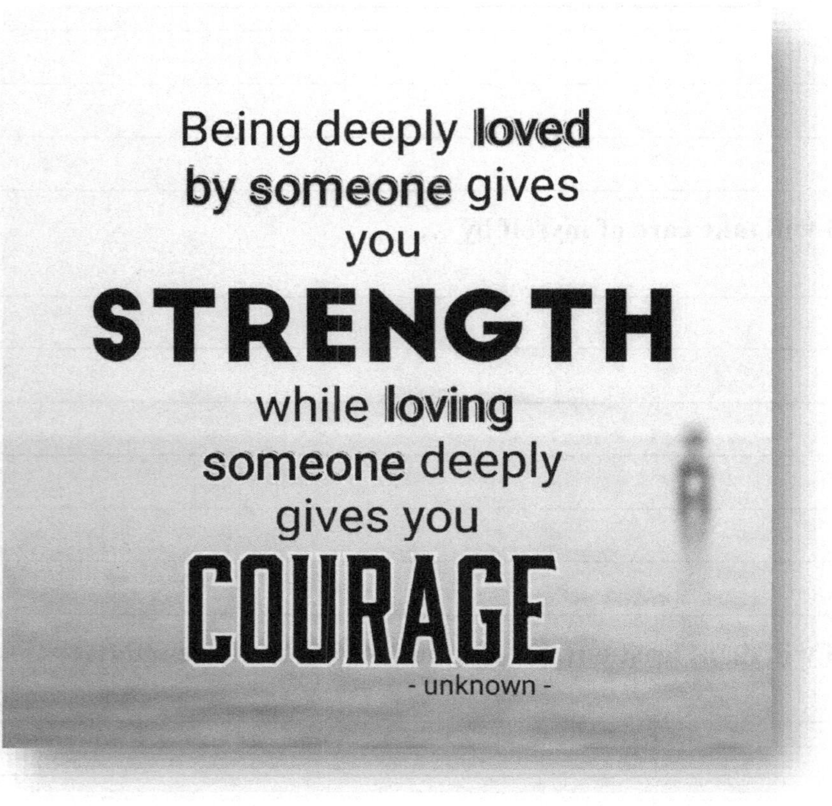
Being deeply loved
by someone gives
you
STRENGTH
while loving
someone deeply
gives you
COURAGE
- unknown -

Date: _____

I am feeling...

_____

_____

_____

_____

_____

_____

_____

_____

_____

_____

_____

_____

_____

_____

_____

_____

_____

_____

_____

_____

_____

_____

I am grateful for...

_____

_____

_____

_____

_____

_____

I will take care of myself by ...

_____

_____

_____

_____

_____

_____

I will do at least one act of kindness for someone today.

_____

_____

_____

_____

_____

_____

_____

"Courage is not the absence of fear but the ability to act despite the presence of fear." – Unknown -

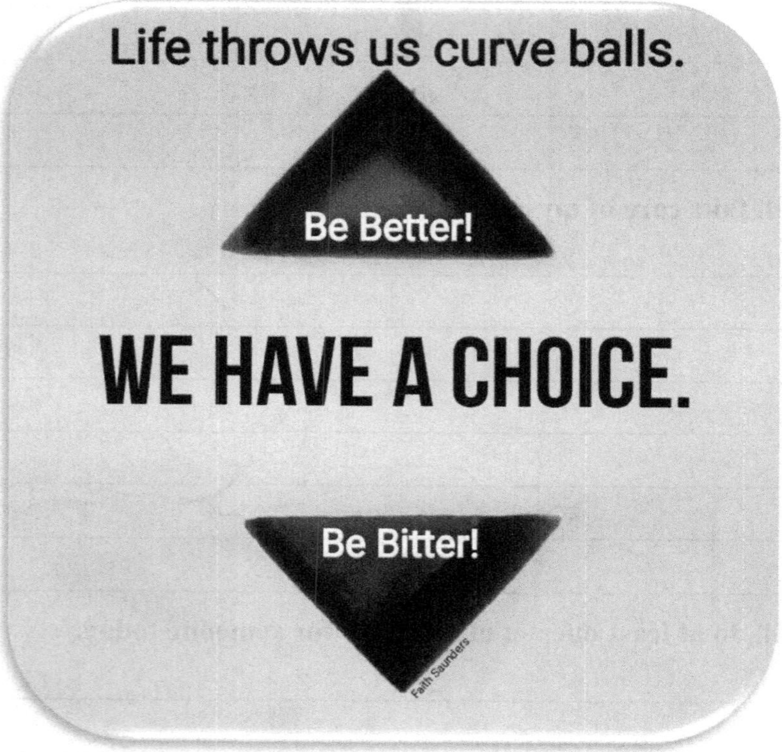
Life throws us curve balls.
Be Better!
WE HAVE A CHOICE.
Be Bitter!
Faith Saunders

Date: _____

I am feeling...

_____
_____
_____
_____
_____
_____
_____
_____
_____
_____
_____
_____
_____
_____
_____
_____
_____
_____
_____
_____
_____
_____
_____
_____
_____
_____
_____

I am grateful for…

_____

_____

_____

_____

_____

_____

_____

_____

I will take care of myself by …

_____

_____

_____

_____

_____

_____

_____

I will do at least one act of kindness for someone today.

_____

_____

_____

_____

_____

_____

_____

_____

"The best way OUT is always through." – Robert Frost –

It's the

little

things that make life

BIG.

-Unknown -

Date: _____

I am feeling…

_____
_____
_____
_____
_____
_____
_____
_____
_____
_____
_____
_____
_____
_____
_____
_____
_____
_____
_____
_____
_____
_____
_____
_____
_____

I am grateful for...

_____

_____

_____

_____

_____

_____

_____

I will take care of myself by ...

_____

_____

_____

_____

_____

_____

I will do at least one act of kindness for someone today.

_____

_____

_____

_____

_____

_____

*There is **ALWAYS** something to be thankful for.*

I wonder what's next?

CURIOSITY
Millions saw the apple fall, only Newton asked WHY.
- Bernard Baruch –

Date: ____________________

I am feeling…

I am grateful for...

_____

_____

_____

_____

_____

_____

I will take care of myself by ...

_____

_____

_____

_____

_____

I will do at least one act of kindness for someone today.

_____

_____

_____

_____

_____

Curiosity can open doors!

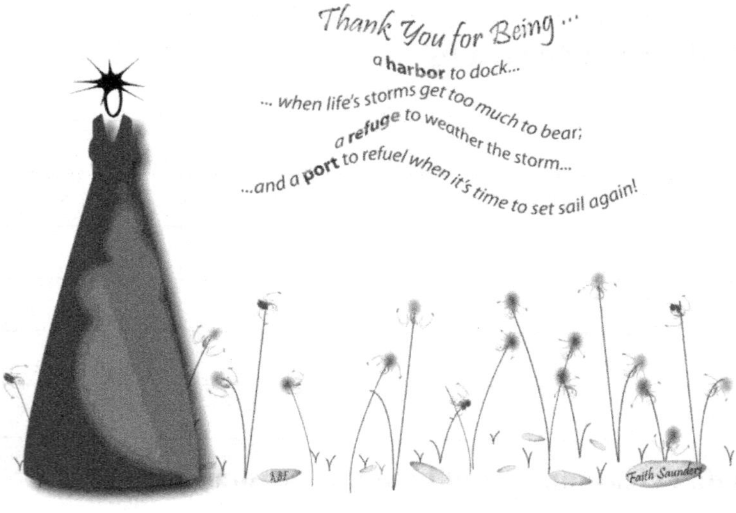
Thank You for Being ...
a harbor to dock...
... when life's storms get too much to bear;
a refuge to weather the storm...
...and a port to refuel when it's time to set sail again!
Faith Saunders

Date: _____

I am feeling...

_____

_____

_____

_____

_____

_____

_____

_____

_____

_____

_____

_____

_____

_____

_____

_____

_____

_____

_____

_____

_____

_____

_____

I am grateful for...

_____

_____

_____

_____

_____

_____

_____

I will take care of myself by ...

_____

_____

_____

_____

_____

_____

I will do at least one act of kindness for someone today.

_____

_____

_____

_____

_____

_____

"You have not touched the tip of the iceberg. There is so much about you that you have yet to uncover." – Faith Saunders -

~Woman Defined ~

I am a person, A WOMAN!
With many creative outlets
~Writer, poet, artist, speaker, actress, dancer~
Some I have yet to uncover!
Try to see me for who I am!
A complex, unique and special
I-N-D-I-V-I-D-U-A-L!
With many emotions, many roles,
and many creative outlets
So please ... DON'T put me in a box!

Faith Saunders

Date: _____

I am feeling...

_____

_____

_____

_____

_____

_____

_____

_____

_____

_____

_____

_____

_____

_____

_____

_____

_____

_____

_____

_____

_____

_____

_____

_____

I am grateful for...

_____

_____

_____

_____

_____

_____

_____

I will take care of myself by ...

_____

_____

_____

_____

_____

_____

I will do at least one act of kindness for someone today.

_____

_____

_____

_____

_____

_____

Wellness includes our physical, emotional, financial, spiritual, occupational and social wellbeing. Which is your strongest one?

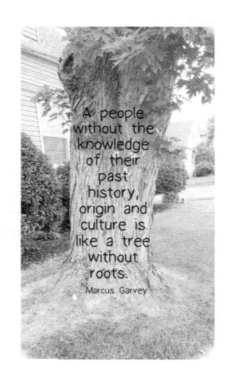

A people without the knowledge of their past history, origin and culture is like a tree without roots.

Marcus Garvey

Date: _____

I am feeling…

_____

_____

_____

_____

_____

_____

_____

_____

_____

_____

_____

_____

_____

_____

_____

_____

_____

_____

_____

_____

_____

_____

I am grateful for...

_____

_____

_____

_____

_____

_____

I will take care of myself by ...

_____

_____

_____

_____

_____

_____

I will do at least one act of kindness for someone today.

_____

_____

_____

_____

_____

_____

What legacy do you want to leave behind?

-

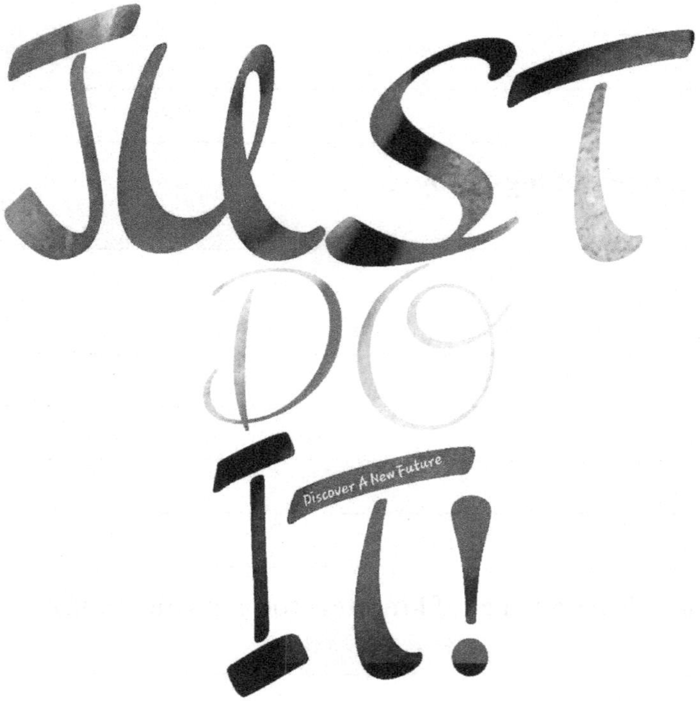
JUST
DO
IT!
Discover A New Future

Date: _____

I am feeling...

_____
_____
_____
_____
_____
_____
_____
_____
_____
_____
_____
_____
_____
_____
_____
_____
_____
_____
_____
_____
_____
_____
_____
_____

I am grateful for...

_____

_____

_____

_____

_____

_____

_____

I will take care of myself by ...

_____

_____

_____

_____

_____

_____

I will do at least one act of kindness for someone today.

_____

_____

_____

_____

_____

_____

Stop procrastinating! Just take action and DO IT!

HOPE is putting faith to work when doubting would be easier. *~Unknown* We should not let our fears hold us back from pursuing our HOPES. *~ John F. Kennedy* Once you choose HOPE, anything's possible. *~ Christopher Reeve~* Things never go so well that one should have no fear, and never so ill that one should have no HOPE. *~ Turkish Proverb ~* HOPE sees the invisible, feels the intangible and achieves the im-possible. *Unknown*

HOPE is the companion of power, and mother of success; for who so hopes strongly has within him the gift of miracles. *Samuel Smiles ~*

Never deprive someone of HOPE - it may be all they have *Unknown ~* When the world says, 'Give up,' HOPE whispers, 'Try it one more time.' *Unknown ~* HOPE never abandons you, you abandon it. *~ George Weinberg ~* HOPE is grief's best music. *Anonymous ~* Keep HOPE alive each day!

Choose your favorite HOPE quote. Write it below.

_____

_____

Date: _____

I am feeling...

_____
_____
_____
_____
_____
_____
_____
_____
_____
_____
_____
_____
_____
_____
_____
_____
_____
_____
_____
_____
_____
_____
_____
_____
_____

I am grateful for...

_____

_____

_____

_____

_____

_____

_____

I will take care of myself by ...

_____

_____

_____

_____

_____

_____

I will do at least one act of kindness for someone today.

_____

_____

_____

_____

_____

_____

H.O.P.E. = **H**old **O**n. **P**ain **E**nds.
- Unknown -

Every oak tree started out as a couple of nuts who decided to stand their ground.

~ Anonymous ~

Date: _____

I am feeling...

I am grateful for...

_____

_____

_____

_____

_____

_____

I will take care of myself by ...

_____

_____

_____

_____

_____

I will do at least one act of kindness for someone today.

_____

_____

_____

_____

_____

_____

What do you stand for?

"Once I woke up,
I know that I would
not sleep anymore."

- Bruce Frank -

Date: _____

I am feeling…

_____

_____

_____

_____

_____

_____

_____

_____

_____

_____

_____

_____

_____

_____

_____

_____

_____

_____

_____

_____

_____

I am grateful for...

_____

_____

_____

_____

_____

_____

I will take care of myself by ...

_____

_____

_____

_____

_____

I will do at least one act of kindness for someone today.

_____

_____

_____

_____

_____

_____

"Once you become self-aware, you'll discover that you don't need the approval of others anymore." – Faith Saunders -

Thank YOU for ALL that You Do!

Date: _____

I am feeling...

I am grateful for...

_____

_____

_____

_____

_____

_____

_____

I will take care of myself by ...

_____

_____

_____

_____

_____

_____

I will do at least one act of kindness for someone today.

_____

_____

_____

_____

_____

_____

_____

"Thank you is the most heartfelt prayer one can say!"
– Unknown -

We welcome your feedback – it is the only way that we can grow.

Please share your thoughts at

https://tinyurl.com/Journal-To-Wellness

faith@discoveranewfuture.com

or

(201) 608-3004

Journal to Wellness

Made in the USA
Middletown, DE
21 September 2024